THE KIDS' JOKE BOOK

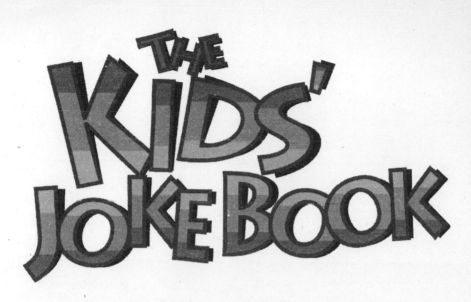

THE KIDS' JOKE BOOK

Hundreds and hundreds of useless, corny, stupid, pointless jokes that you will love to bits !

Collected and Illustrated by

PETER COUPE

Canadian editors
Blair Wilkinson & Madelyn Wilkinson

ARCTURUS

Published by Arcturus Publishing Limited

This edition published 2001

Printed and bound in Finland

ISBN 1 900032 22 8

Contents...

Nutty Names...

What do you call a man who writes joke books for a living?

Poor!

What do you call a man with a cable
coming out of his ear ?

Mike !

★

What do you call a man who does
everything at top speed ?

Max !

★

What do you call the ghost of a
Star Trek character ?

Doctor Spook !

★

What do you call a super hero who
looks after books ?

Conan the Librarian !

★

What do you call an overweight vampire ?

Draculard !

What do you call a woman who works for a lawyer ?

Sue !

★

What do you call a man who goes fishing every weekend ?

Rod !

★

What do you call a teacher with earplugs in ?

Anything you like - he can't hear you !

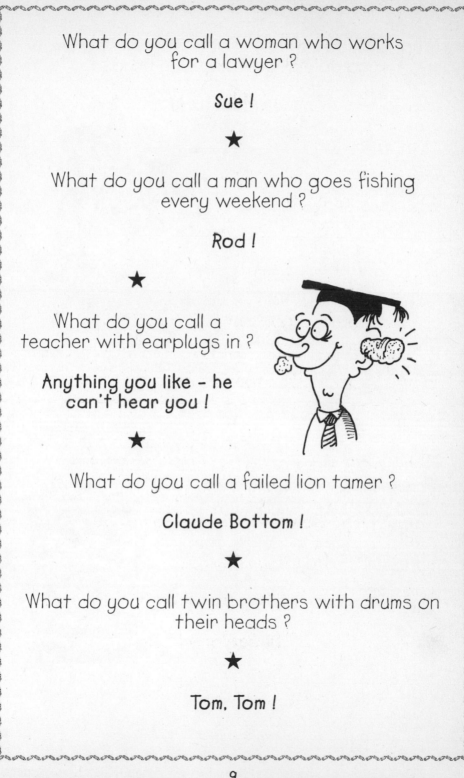

★

What do you call a failed lion tamer ?

Claude Bottom !

★

What do you call twin brothers with drums on their heads ?

★

Tom, Tom !

What do you call a man and woman who show you up in front of your friends ?

Mum and Dad !

★

What do you call a man who likes drawing and painting ?

Art !

★

What do you call a man who does odd jobs and lives just round the corner ?

Andy !

★

Prisoner - It's not my fault. I was given a name that was bound to lead me into crime !

Judge - What is your name ?

Prisoner - Robin Banks !

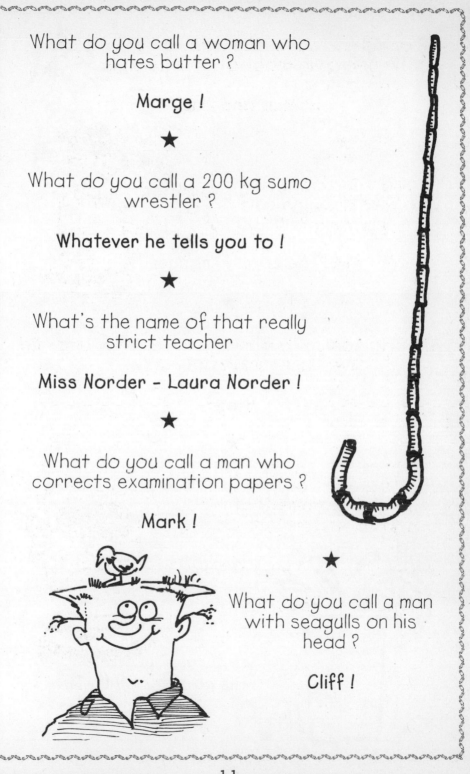

What do you call a woman who hates butter ?

Marge !

★

What do you call a 200 kg sumo wrestler ?

Whatever he tells you to !

★

What's the name of that really strict teacher

Miss Norder - Laura Norder !

★

What do you call a man who corrects examination papers ?

Mark !

★

What do you call a man with seagulls on his head ?

Cliff !

What do you call a woman who only comes out at Christmas?

Carol !

★

What do you call a masked man who lends you money?

The Loan Arranger !

★

What do you call a woman who checks punctuation?

Dot !

★

I call him Bill - he's always asking me for money !

★

Did you hear about the man who used to make his living selling refreshments in the intermission at football games?

His name.......... Alf Time !

What do you call a
Scotsman with his own
computer ?

Mac !

★

What do you call a woman
who can makes pints
disappear in a pub ?

Beatrix !

★

What do you call a man who keeps pet rabbits ?

Warren !

★

What do you call a man who
keeps pet rabbits and
writes epic novels ?

Warren Peace !

★

What do you call a man who
keeps an angry ferret down
his pants ?

Very, very stupid !

13

What do you call the man who stamps the letters at the Post Office ?

Frank !

★

What do you call a man who works in a perfume shop at Christmas ?

Frank in Scents !

★

What do you call a woman having a meal in a restaurant ?

Anita !

★

What do you call a Spanish woman having a meal in a restaurant ?

Juanita !

★

If you really loved me,
You'd let me call you Jack.
Then you could lift my car
and mend the puncture at
the back !

What do you call a girl who has her own car ?

Minnie !

★

What do you call a jogger in a safari park ?

Fast food !

★

What do you call someone with more money than sense ?

My best Pal !

★

The dimmest boy in my class has the same initials as the contents of his head.....M.T.

★

What do you call the man who serves fizzy drinks in your house ?

Pop !

What do you call a man with loads of money ?

Rich !

★

What do you call a fish
that tunes pianos ?

A Piano Tuna !

★

What do you call Mr Smith's half brother ?

Arthur Smith !

★

What do you call a
magician's assistant ?

Trixie !

★

What do you call someone
who never blows his nose ?

Ronnie !

★

What do you call a man who likes to grow flowers, fruit and vegetables ?

Gordon !

★

What do you call the brother and sister who like to build things across rivers ?

Archie and Bridget !

★

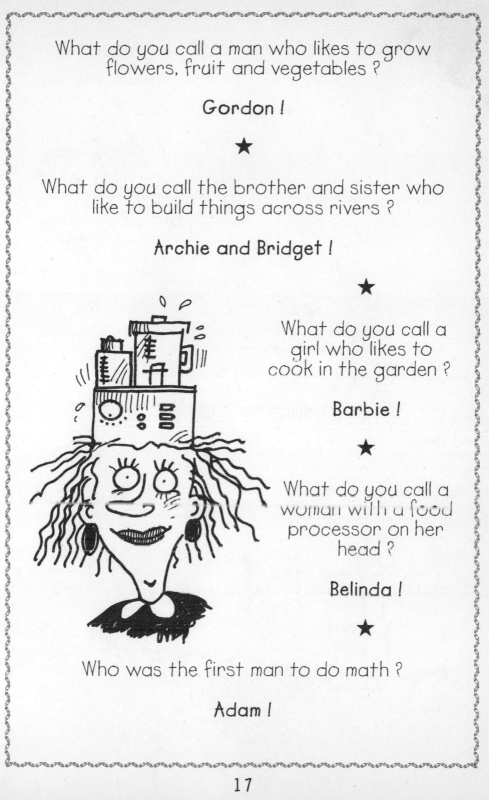

What do you call a girl who likes to cook in the garden ?

Barbie !

★

What do you call a woman with a food processor on her head ?

Belinda !

★

Who was the first man to do math ?

Adam !

What do you call a man who hosts a quiz show at Christmas ?

Santa Clues !

★

What do you call someone who claps when contestants get the right answer ?

Santapplause !

★

What do you call the camel with three humps that fell off the wall and smashed into millions of pieces ?

Humphrey Dumpty !

★

What do you call a man who lies in front of your door all day ?

Matt !

What do you call a girl with lots of suitcases ?

Carrie !

★

What do you call a man that people sit on in meetings ?

The Chairman !

★

That frog is a secret agent - his name's Pond,

James Pond !

★

What do you call a man who slowly runs out of energy ?

Peter !

★

What do you call a girl who never stands up straight ?

Eileen !

What do you call
a girl who lives in
a pond ?

Lily !

★

What do you call
a nun with a
radio on her
head ?

A Transister !

★

What do you call
a teacher who
eats toffees in
class ?

A Chew-tor !

★

What do you call a computer's favourite cake
ingredient ?

Electric currents !

★

What do you call someone that witches go to when they are sick ?

A witch doctor, of course !

★

What do you call a ghost that picks his nose ?

A Bogeyman !

★

What do you call a young bee ?

A Baby !

★

Is it true...
that the man that invented ice came from...

Cuba ?

★

What do you call a man with three legs ?

Nothing - he's certain to catch you if you do !

SHIVER

SHIVER

What do you call a teacher who has a
lot of accidents ?

Miss Hap !

★

What do you call the hairstyle you get from
sticking your head in an oven ?

A Micro - wave !

★

What was the name of the explorer with a
passion for biscuits ?

Captain Cookie !

★

What do you call the boy who is also a goat ?

Billy !

★

What do you call the woman who brings him to
school every day ?

His Nanny !

★

School
Screams...

Teacher - You should have been here at
9 o'clock this morning !

Pupil - Why, did something happen ?

English Teacher - Sally, do you like Kipling ?

Sally - I don't know, Sir, I've never eaten one !

★

My last school was so rough they didn't have a school photograph - they sent home identikit pictures instead !

★

Science Teacher - Gary, do you know what Copper Nitrate is ?

Gary - Yes Sir, it's what they pay policemen on night duty !

★

History Teacher - Martin, where would I find Hadrian's wall ?

Martin - Wherever Hadrian left it, Sir !

★

Maths Teacher - Carol, why have you brought a picture of Henry the eighth in with you ?

Carol - You told us to bring a ruler in with us today !

Teacher - name one of Noah's children.

Pupil - Joan of Arc ?

★

And... for all those who were late this morning because they stayed up to watch the hockey... we're going to make School more like hockey...

you will all stay behind and do extra time tonight as a penalty !

★

Maths teacher - Blenkinsop, can you tell me the 9 times table please ?

Blenkinsop - You asked me that yesterday, don't tell me you've forgotten it already !

★

Teacher - You're on English level 4 aren't you, Smith ?

Smith - Yes.

Teacher - Then take this English level 2 book for your father or he's never going to be able to catch up and do your homework properly !

Of course in my day you only had the one choice for school dinners...................

.............Like it or lump it !

★

Where do Martians go to train to be teachers ?

Mooniversity !

★

I think my maths teacher is in love with me...

How do you work that out ?

...she puts red kisses all over my homework !

★

What's the best snake to take into a maths lesson ?

An adder !

I would have done my homework, but.....

I didn't have any pocket money left, and my sister always demands cash in advance.....

My dad was working late, and he has all the brains in the family.....

My pen ran out and I spent all night looking for an inkwell.....

★

What is a history teacher's favourite fruit ?

Dates !

★

Please Miss, is it true that the French only ever eat one egg for breakfast ?

What makes you ask that ?

Because yesterday you said that in France, one egg is un oeuf !

★

Did you hear about the teacher who had to wear sunglasses in the classroom ?

He had extremely bright pupils !

★

Anxious parent - What do you think my son will be when he has finished all his exams ?

Teacher - An old age pensioner !

★

How many teachers does it take to work the photocopier ?

Who cares, as long as it keeps them out of the classroom !

Principal - You boy, stop running around like that ! Don't you know who I am ?

Pupil - There's a man here who doesn't even know who he is !

Why do swimming teachers like elephants ?

Because they never forget their trunks !

★

*We've got a new drama teacher -
she's a real class act !*

★

Principal - That's Hodgkiss, the school bully.

Visitor - How dreadful, can't you do anything
to stop him ?

**Principal - Certainly not, or I'd never get the
teachers back to the classrooms after lunch
break !**

★

Who is a teacher's
favourite actor ?

Michael Caine !

★

*Eric should make an
excellent train
driver, as he has
more experience of
lines than any other
pupil in the school !*

Our cooking teacher knows his onions...

Our P.E. teacher thinks we're a real shower...

Our last math teacher was taken away...

**Our music teacher never accepts notes
from home...**

★

Where do new teachers come from ?

They're produced on an assembly line !

★

What were the names of
the very first teachers ?

Miss and Sir !

★

Teacher - Is your father helping you with your
homework ?

Pupil - No, sir, if anything he knows even less
than I do !

★

Well, son, how did you find the math exam ?

Unfortunately, it wasn't lost !

Teacher - Smith, give me a sentence with the word politics in it.

Smith - My pet parrot swallowed the alarm clock and now Polly ticks !

★

What's the best way to tell your math teacher that you have forgotten to do your homework - again ?

From a great distance !

★

Teacher - If your father gave you $5.00 pocket money and your mother gave you $10.00, what would you have ?

Pupil - Someone else's parents !

★

Did you hear about the cross eyed teacher who had to retire ?

He couldn't control his pupils !

Teacher - Well, at least I know that no-one in the school football team will ever start smoking.

Principal - How do you work that out ?

Teacher - Because they always lose their matches !

★

Our School cook was arrested for cruelty - she was caught beating eggs, battering fish fingers and whipping cream !

★

John - I bet our chemistry teacher could cure your insomnia mum...

Mum - Why, is he a doctor as well ?

John - No, but as soon as he starts to speak half the class fall asleep !

★

Teacher - Are you sending Gary to boarding school ?

Parent - Yes. His report says he is always bored !

★

Games Teacher - Read these books and they will help you get fit - they are exercise books !

Why are math teachers so good at solving detective stories ?

Because they can tell when all the clues add up !

★

Teacher -How many letters in the alphabet ?

Pupil - 25 !

Teacher - How do you work that out ?

Pupil - Well, it's Christmas next week, so there's Noel !

★

Principal - Why did you call Mulder and Scully into the school ?

Pupil - I looked into the school kitchen and saw an unidentified frying object !

★

Teacher -Jenkins, what's the difference between an elephant and my desk ?

Jenkins - Don't know sir.

Teacher - In that case I think I'll send someone else to put these books in my desk drawers !

Teacher - I just don't understand how one person can make so many mistakes in their homework !

Pupil - Oh I can't take all the credit, sir, my Dad did most of it !

★

We sent our teacher's photograph to a lonely hearts club...

They sent it straight back - they said they weren't THAT lonely !

★

How can you tell when a teacher is in a good mood ?

No, I don't know either !

★

What do you call a teacher with a pile of sports equipment on his head ?

Jim !

★

What is the robot teacher's favourite part of the day ?

Assembly !

What do math teachers do when their sinks get blocked ?

They work it out with a pencil !

★

What do cannibals have for school dinners ?

Snake and pygmy pie, with chimps and beings !

★

What do you call a boy who only just gets to school on time every day ?

Justin !

★

Did you hear about the math teacher who wanted an Italian take away, but was divided about whether to have additional cheese !

★

Our technology teacher left to try and make something of himself !

★

Who's your favourite teacher ?

The Finnish one !

We haven't got any Finnish teachers !

Yes we have. Every day she says "Finish what you're doing and go home !

★

Mum - How did you do at school today ?

John - Great ! The teacher told me I was a moron !

Mum -And it's not as if you come from a religious family !

★

Steve - I wish MY dad would help me with my homework like yours does !

Joe - I wish your dad would help me as well. I got 3 out of 25 and another detention thanks to mine !

Knock, Knock...

Knock, Knock...
Who's there ?
Giraffe...
Giraffe Who ?
Giraffe to sit in front of me
at the cinema ?

Knock, knock
Who's there ?
Amanda
Amanda who ?
Amanda last step - open the door !

★

Knock, knock
Who's there ?
Dell
Dell who ?
Dell never know I was here if you don't
tell them !

★

Knock, knock
Who's there ?
Toodle
Toodle who ?
Where are you going - I only just got here !

★

Knock, knock
Who's there ?
Paul
Paul who ?
Paul the door open and you'll see !

★

Knock Knock...
Who's there ?
Joanna...
Joanna who ?
Joanna stop asking stupid questions
and let me in !

★

Knock Knock...
Who's there ?
Ant...
Ant who ?
Ant I told you already ?

★

Knock Knock Knock...
Who's there ?
Moses...
Moses who ?
Moses if I knock 3 times you'll let me in !

★

Knock Knock...
Who's there ?
Tim...
Tim who ?
T-I-M-B-E-R !@*!!

★

Knock Knock...
Who's there ?
Kent...
Kent who ?
Kent you fix the doorbell ?

★

Knock Knock...
Who's there ?
Yul...
Yul who ?
Yul never know if you don't
open the door will you ? !

★

Knock Knock...
Who's there ?
Your math teacher...
hello...hello....Is anyone
there...?

★

Knock Knock...
Who's there ?
Isabel...
Isabel who ?
Isabel a legal
requirement on a bicycle ?

★

Knock Knock...
Who's there ?
Superman...
Superman who ?
You know I can't reveal my secret identity !

★

Knock Knock...
Who's there ?
Dooby Doobid...
Dooby Doobid who ?
Ah ! A Frank Sinatra fan !

★

Knock Knock...
Who's there ?
Doctor...
Doctor who ?
Have you seen my Tardis !?

Knock Knock...
Who's there ?
Tish...
Tish who ?
Bless you !

★

Knock Knock...
Who's there ?
Twitter...
Twitter who ?
You got an owl in there ?

★

Knock Knock...
Who's there ?
Snow...
Snow who ?
Snow use - I can't remember

Knock Knock...
Who's there?
Snow...
Snow who ?
Snow joke being out here
in the cold, let me in !

★

Knock Knock...
Who's there ?
Nona...
Nona who ?
Nona your business !

★

Knock Knock...
Who's there ?
Adolf...
Adolf who ?
Adolf ball hit me in de mouf !

Knock Knock...
Who's there ?
Alec...
Alec who ?
Alec to see you guess !

★

Knock Knock...
Who's there ?
Les...
Les who ?
Les cut the small talk - just open the door !

★

Knock Knock...
Who's there ?
Wendy...
Wendy who ?
Wendy red red robin goes bob bob
bobbin along...

★

Knock Knock...
Who's there ?
Guess...
Guess who ?
Hang on, haven't we got this mixed up
somehow ?

Knock Knock...
Who's there ?
Kungf...
Kungf who ?
No need to threaten
me !

★

Knock Knock...
Who's there ?
Marky...
Marky who ?
Markys stuck in the
keyhole,
can you open it
from your side ?

★

Knock Knock...
Who's there ?
Knock Knock...
Who's there ?
Knock Knock...
Just a minute I'll
open the door -
Yes, can I help you ?
I've called to collect
my new hearing aid !

★

Knock Knock...
Who's there ?
Police...
Police who ?
Police let me in, I'm freezing out here !

★

Knock Knock...
Who's there ?
Pat...
Pat who ?
**Actually it's Steve, I was just doing
an impersonation of Pat !**

★

Knock Knock...
Who's there ?
Joe...
Joe who ?
**Joe always have to
ask me that question ?**

★

Knock Knock...
Who's there ?
The Cilla...
The Cilla who ?
**The Cilla beggar who's
forgotten her key again !**

Knock Knock...
Who's there ?
Your math teacher...
This is a recording...there's no one here
at the moment !

★

Knock Knock...
Who's there ?
Jim...
Jim who ?
Jim mind if I stay here tonight ?

★

Knock Knock...
Who's there ?
Aliens...
Aliens who ?
**Just how many
Aliens
do you know ?**

Knock Knock...
Who's there ?
Boo...
Boo who ?
No need to get upset, it's only a game !

★

Knock Knock...
Who's there ?
Mike...
Mike who ?
**Mike car won't start, can I
come in and phone the garage ?**

★

Knock Knock...
Who's there ?
Carol...
Carol who ?
**Carol singers - you must
have heard us we've been
at it for 20 minutes !**

★

Knock Knock...
Who's there ?
Phil...
Phil who ?
Phil this bag with money,
I'm a burglar !

★

Knock Knock...
Who's there ?
The man from next door...
The man from next door who ?
The man from next door who has clearly come
home to the wrong house, sorry !

★

Knock Knock...
Who's there ?
Luke...
Luke who ?
Luke, stop messing about
and let me in !

Knock Knock...
Who's there ?
Alec...
Alec who ?
Alec your front door !

★

Knock Knock...
Who's there ?
Haydn...
Haydn who ?
Haydn like it at all !

★

Knock Knock...
Who's there ?
Ivan...
Ivan who ?
Ivan to come in - open the door !

★

Knock Knock...
Who's there ?
Josie...
Josie who ?
Josie any reason to keep me
waiting out here ?

★

Knock Knock...
Who's there ?
The Spice Girls...
Come in, come in, how rude of me to keep you
waiting...

★

Knock Knock...
Who's there ?
Jeanie...
Jeanie who ?
Jeanie comprend pas - je suis Francais !

★

Knock Knock...
Who's there ?
Bill...
Bill who ?
Bill-ieve it or not this is a joke !

★

Knock Knock...
Who's there ?
Bert...
Bert who ?
Bert surely you recognise my voice !

★

Knock Knock...
Who's there ?
Ernie...
Ernie who ?
Ernie chance of you opening the door ?

★

Knock Knock...
Who's there ?
Norman...
Norman who ?
**Norman gets past this door
without your permission do they ? !**

★

Knock Knock...
Who's there ?
Ivor...
Ivor who ?
Ivor key of my own now !

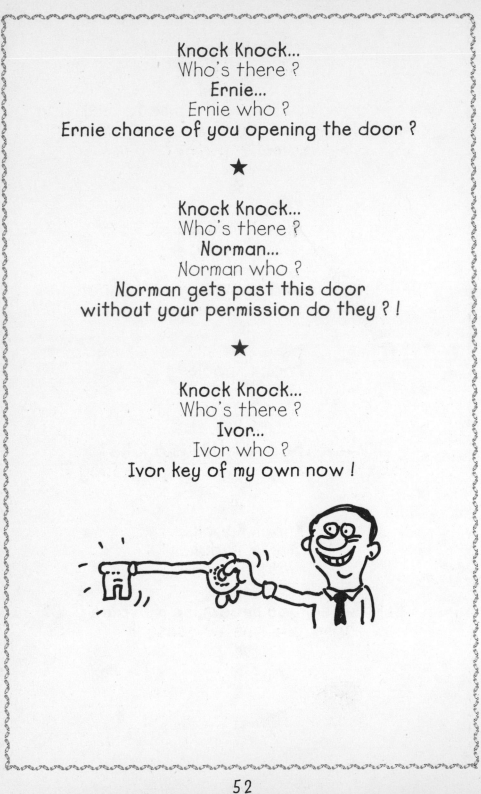

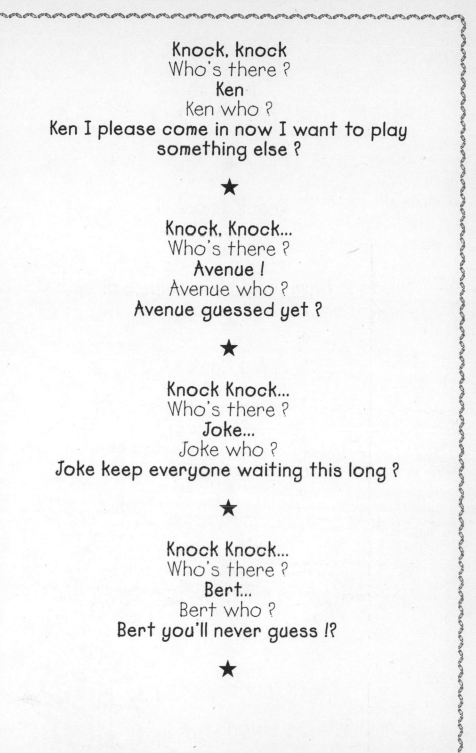

Knock, knock
Who's there ?
Ken
Ken who ?
Ken I please come in now I want to play
something else ?

★

Knock, Knock...
Who's there ?
Avenue !
Avenue who ?
Avenue guessed yet ?

★

Knock Knock...
Who's there ?
Joke...
Joke who ?
Joke keep everyone waiting this long ?

★

Knock Knock...
Who's there ?
Bert...
Bert who ?
Bert you'll never guess !?

★

Knock, knock
Who's there ?
The Witch
The Witch who ?
Bless you !

★

Knock, knock
Who's there ?
Maddona
Maddona who ?
Maddona have to stand out here all night !

★

Knock, knock
Who's there ?
Gunga Din
Gunga Din who ?
Gunga Din the door's locked !

★

Knock, knock
Who's there ?
Nige
Nige who ?
Nige who believe it's me ?

★

Knock Knock...
Go away ! I'm reading
the next section !

Animal Antics...

Looks like Reindeer !

What do you call a goat who robs banks ?

Billy the Kid !

★

If cows get milked - what do goats get ?

Butted !

★

*If a house mouse sleeps in a house
and a field mouse sleeps in a field
do dormice sleep in dorms ?*

★

Where do rabbits go when they want
something to read ?

Buck Shops !

★

Rabbit - How do I know this TV will work when
I get it home ?

Shopkeeper -It comes with a full Warrenty !

★

Name a comedian that dogs really like...

...Ronnie Barker !

Why do elephants
paint their toenails
red ?

So they can hide in
Cherry trees !

★

Hickory Dickory Dock,
The horse ran up the clock.

Anybody need any firewood ?

★

Why is the sky so high ?

So birds don't bump their heads !

★

What goes... 'Now you see me, now you don't ?'

A Zebra using a crosswalk !

★

What will you get if you sit under a cow ?

A pat on the head !

When Mary had a little lamb
The doctor was surprised
But when Old Macdonald had a farm
He couldn't believe his eyes !

★

What do porcupines eat with their cheese ?

Prickled onions !

★

What do you get if you
cross a cow with a camel ?

Lumpy custard !

★

How do you stop rabbits digging up your
garden ?

Easy - take their spades away !

★

What was the title of the Shakespeare play
about pigs ?

Hamlet !

We call our dog Locksmith because every now and again he makes a bolt for the door !

★

Why are you taking that snake into the math exam ?

It's an adder !

★

How many elephants can you get into a car ?

Four. 2 in the front seats and 2 in the back seats !

★

How many hippos can you get into a car ?

Four ?

Don't be silly ! There are 4 elephants in it already !

★

Amateur Lion Taming

by

Claude Bottom

What do you call an elephant in a telephone booth ?

Whatever you like - it will be stuck so it can't chase you !

★

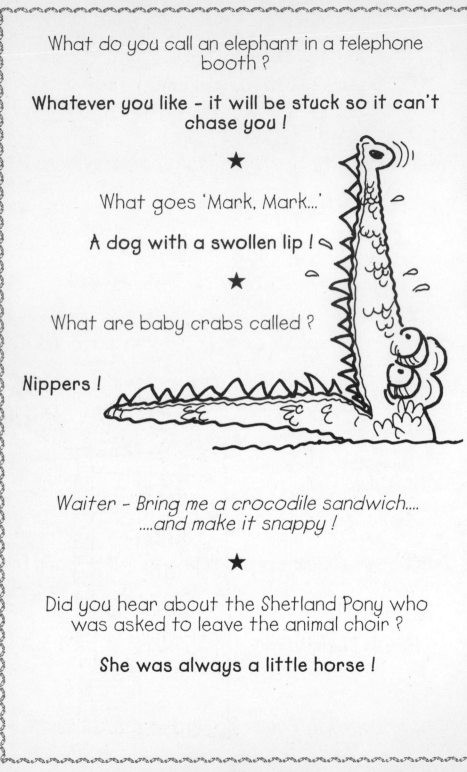

What goes 'Mark, Mark...'

A dog with a swollen lip !

★

What are baby crabs called ?

Nippers !

*Waiter - Bring me a crocodile sandwich....
....and make it snappy !*

★

Did you hear about the Shetland Pony who was asked to leave the animal choir ?

She was always a little horse !

Police are looking for a criminal octopus...

He is well armed and dangerous !

★

What lies at the bottom of the sea and shivers ?

A nervous wreck !

★

What's the fastest fish in the lake ?

A motor Pike !

★

What does your cat eat for breakfast ?

Mine eats Mice Crispies !

★

Did you know that alligators eat beans for breakfast ?

Human Beans of course !

HUMAN
BEANS
IN
TOMATO
SAUCE

Noah's Ark was able to find its way about at night because it had been fitted with floodlights !

★

Why do bees hum ?

Because they have forgotten the words !

★

Where do you take an injured bee ?

To the waspital !

...just as you would take an injured pony to the horsepital !

★

Why do railway porters like elephants ?

Because they always carry their own trunks !

What has 10 legs, 3 heads but only 2 arms ?

A man and a dog sitting on a zebra !

★

What's grey and zooms through the jungle at 70 miles an hour ?

An elephant on a motor bike !

★

Why should you never play cards for money in the jungle ?

Because there are too many Cheetahs about !

★

What vegetable do you get if you cross a sheepdog with a bunch of daffodils ?

A collie - flower !

★

Why is the sky blue ?

So birds know there not flying upside down !

What game do ponies play ?

Stable tennis !

★

What's green and highly dangerous ?

A frog with a machine gun !

★

Why did the dinosaur cross the road ?

Because chickens hadn't been invented
in those days !

★

Why did the snake cross the road ?

Because it couldn't use
the footbridge !

★

Is that budgie expensive ?

No, sir, it's going cheep !

What do you call a rich trendy elephant ?

A member of the jumbo jet set !

★

Why did the duck cross the road ?

It was the chicken's day off !

★

Why do eagles go to church ?

Because they are birds of prey !

★

Why do elephants have wrinkles ?

Because they hate ironing !

How do you know if an elephant has
been in your fridge ?

They leave footprints in the butter !

What creature comes in handy in the car ?

A windshield Viper !

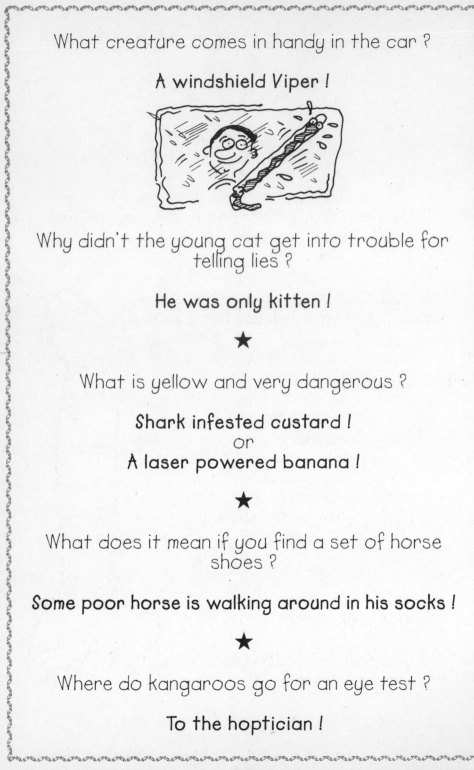

Why didn't the young cat get into trouble for telling lies ?

He was only kitten !

★

What is yellow and very dangerous ?

Shark infested custard !
or
A laser powered banana !

★

What does it mean if you find a set of horse shoes ?

Some poor horse is walking around in his socks !

★

Where do kangaroos go for an eye test ?

To the hoptician !

I can't do it, you can't do it, the farmer can't do it...

...what is it ?

Milk chocolate !

★

Another name for parrot food - **pollyfilla !**

★

Did you hear about the dog who was too lazy to dig up his bone ?

He was bone idle !

★

How many sheep does it take to make a sweater ?

I didn't even know that sheep could knit !

★

Why are elephants grey ?

So you can tell them apart from strawberries !

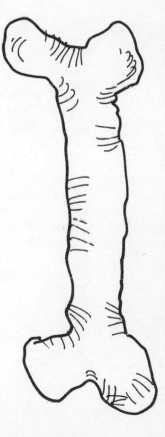

Why does a giraffe have such a long neck ?

Have you ever smelled a giraffe's feet !?

★

Bullfighting
for
beginners

by

Matt. A. Dores

★

When sheep are cold they gather in a big circle
and a few sheep in the centre make a lot of
noise and this keeps everyone else warm...

...this is called central bleating !

★

What do the police have to have before they
can come into your home looking for escaped
parrots ?

A perch warrant !

★

What do you call a sheep with a machine gun ?

Lambo !

What does a cat rest his head on in bed ?

A caterpiller !

★

What sort of cat sells wood ?

A Catalogue !

What part of a car can be used to change cats into something else ?

The catalytic converter !

★

What bulls hide on the riverbank waiting to charge at you ?

Bullrushes !

★

If you go to the doctor because you are a little hoarse, what is he likely to give you ?

Cough Stirrup !

★

Have you changed the water in the goldfish bowl ?

No, they haven't drunk the water I put in yesterday yet !

★

What is a cat's favourite TV programme ?

The Mews at Ten !

★

I'd like a tube of cat glue please !

What on earth is that for ?

Well, I always thought that cats came in one piece - but someone told me you have to buy them as kits !

★

Monster Madness...

Eat your sprouts, they'll put
colour in your cheeks.

But I don't want green cheeks !

What do vampires buy every week ?

The Clottery Tickets !

★

What should you take if a monster invites you for dinner ?

Someone who can't run as fast as you !

★

Why do vampires have to write so many letters ?

They have to reply to their fang clubs !

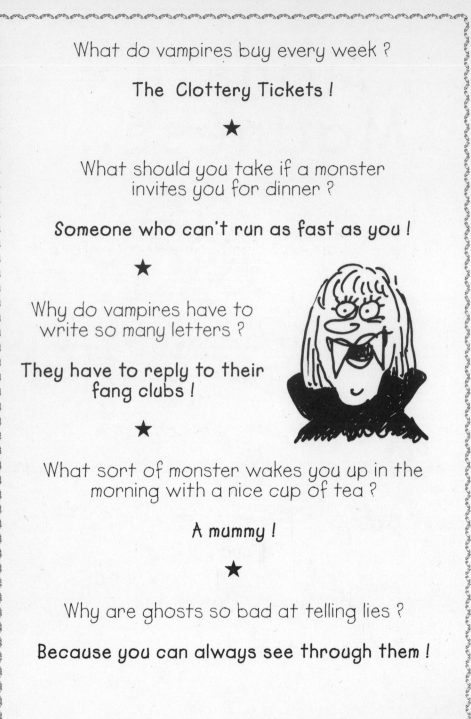

★

What sort of monster wakes you up in the morning with a nice cup of tea ?

A mummy !

★

Why are ghosts so bad at telling lies ?

Because you can always see through them !

The Haunted House

by

Hugo First

★

Mummy, what is a vampire ?

Be quiet dear and drink your blood before it clots !

★

What do you call an evil,
8 foot tall, green,
hairy monster ?

Whatever he tells you to !

★

What is a monster's favourite handicraft ?

Tie and Die !

★

What is a monster's favourite game ?

Hide and Shriek !

★

Did you see that wolf ?

Where ?

No, it was just an ordinary one !

★

What's the name of that very
scary all girl band ?

You mean the Spice Ghouls !

★

It's no good locking your door - monsters can
always get in !

They have a set of skeleton keys !

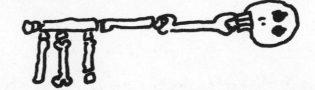

Doctor, said the cannibal, I have this terrible stomach ache !

You must have eaten someone who disagreed with you !

★

A vampire's coffin fell off the back of a truck and started rolling down a steep hill. The vampire knew exactly what to do. He went into a local drugstore and asked if they had any sore throat sweets to stop his coffin !

★

Where do vampires keep their savings ?

In a blood bank !

★

Did you hear about the baby monster who had hundreds of little holes all over his face ?

He was learning to eat with a fork !

★

Why do vampires take their football so seriously ?

Because there is always so much at stake !

Where do ghosts practise frightening people ?

At swooniversity !

★

What do ghosts write their letters on?

Type - frighters !

★

How do mummies keep a secret ?

They keep it under wraps !

★

What do you call a monster who never blows his nose ?

The bogeyman !

★

Why do skeletons rub themselves all over with towels when they've been swimming ?

To get bone dry !

★

What is a sea monsters favourite fastfood ?

Fish and ships

★

I know a vampire who spends all morning
writing letters...

Well, he has to reply to his fang mail !

Menu

Sean cocktail

or

Dawn on the cob

followed by

I scream !
(and so would you if you had been there !)

★

What's the difference between a monster
and an omelette ?

One is full of yolks, the other full of folks !

What sort of horses do monsters ride?

Night mares !

★

When a monster's hungry and needs to be fed,
it's no good hiding under the bed !
He'll roll you in the mattress,
till you're buried like a mole,
then chomp you down in two big bites,
like a giant sausage roll !

★

Why was the monster's head sticky ?

Because he styled his hair with a honey comb !

What did the monster say when it saw
someone going past on a mountain bike ?

Ah ! Meals on wheels !

★

What is a vampire's favourite soup ?

Scream of mushroom !

★

Monster - Waiter, this is ordinary spaghetti
- I ordered worms !

**Waiter - Ah, I wondered why the man on the
table next to you was being sick in the toilet !**

★

Sally - What is the difference between a
monster and a digestive biscuit ?

Jim - I don't know.

**Sally - Have you ever tried dunking a
monster in your tea?**

★

A ghost went into a pub at midnight and asked the barman for a whisky. "Sorry sir," replied the barman, "we aren't allowed to serve spirits after closing time."

★

Party games for monsters...

Pass the person
and
swallow the leader !

★

What sort of monsters have wavy hair ?

Sea monsters !

★

What do you have to get if you invite monsters round to your house for a party ?

A new house !

What did the vampire say when it saw the queue at the doctor's surgery?

Necks please!

★

What do Hungarian ghosts eat?

Ghoulash!

★

What position do ghosts play on hockey teams?

Ghoultenders!

★

What do you call a relaxed ghost?

Ghoul as a cucumber!

★

What do you call a haunted set square?

A trian-ghoul!

★

What is a monster's favourite soup ?

Any flavour, as long as it's a hearty meal !

★

Why do travelling salesmen always try to
sell things to vampires ?

Because they know they are suckers !

★

Where was Frankenstein's head made ?

Bolton !

★

Why does Dracula wear bright red braces ?

To hold his trousers up !

What sound do baby ghosts make when they cry ?

Boo Hoo !
or
they wail !

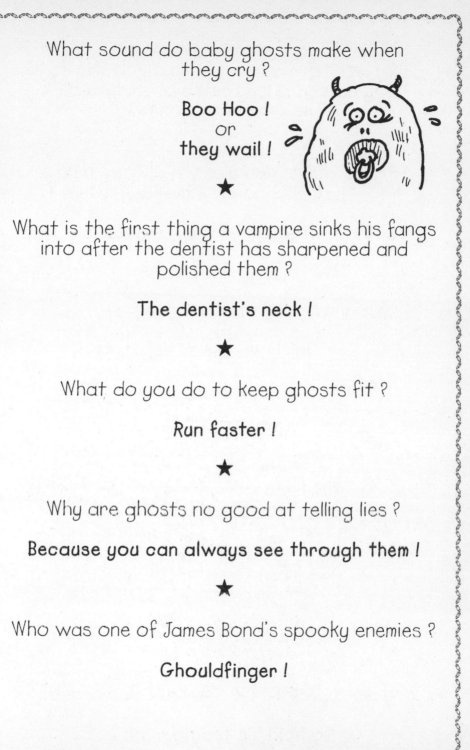

★

What is the first thing a vampire sinks his fangs into after the dentist has sharpened and polished them ?

The dentist's neck !

★

What do you do to keep ghosts fit ?

Run faster !

★

Why are ghosts no good at telling lies ?

Because you can always see through them !

★

Who was one of James Bond's spooky enemies ?

Ghouldfinger !

What sort of vampires prey on elephants ?

The very stupid ones !

★

What do ghosts do in the countryside ?

They go fox haunting !

★

What do you do to keep ghosts fit ?

Call in an exercisist !

★

A new ghost was sitting in bed reading when an old ghost walked through the wall and into his room.
"It's no good,' said the new ghost, "I still don't understand how you do it"
"Watch," said the old ghost, "and I'll go through it again !"

★

What tune to ghosts sing their babies to sleep with ?

Ghoulden slumbers !

Fishy Foolishness...

Which fish runs the undersea mafia ?

The Codfather !

Why are Herrings such healthy fish ?

**Because you never see them ill,
only cured !**

★

What sort of fish go to heaven when they die ?

Angel fish !

★

*Roses are red,
violets are blue,
you look like a
trout, and you
smell like one
too !*

★

*If you use a
skunk to catch fish you always
catch them hook, line and stinker !*

★

What do you get in a takeaway next to a
power station ?

Nuclear fission chips !

Which sea creatures do you need for a game of fish?

Prawns!

★

Where do dolphins learn?

In Schools, of course!

★

Where do baby fish go?

To Plaice-school!

★

What would you eat in an sunken pirate ship take away?

Pizzas of eight!

How do fish go on holiday ?

They take the whale-way !

★

Which sea creatures never go to parties in
case they are eaten by mistake ?

Jelly fish !

What do you call a naughty little fish ?

Minnow the minx !

★

Knock, knock...
Who's there ?
Plaice...
Plaice who ?
**Plaice let me in,
I'm wet through !**

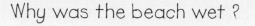

Why was the beach wet ?

Because the sea weed !

★

Why are some shellfish
always bad tempered ?

**They can't help it -
they were born crabby
!**

★

Where do fish like going for their holidays ?

Finland !

★

How do fish know exactly
what everything weighs ?

**They always have a set
of scales on them !**

★

What do sharks eat at parties ?

**Fish-cakes
Jelly-fish
and
Sandwiches**

★

Where do whales get weighed ?

At a whale - weigh station !

★

What do fish drink ?

Water of course, they can't use bottle openers !

★

What do fish use to stop getting sunburned ?

Sun tan ocean !

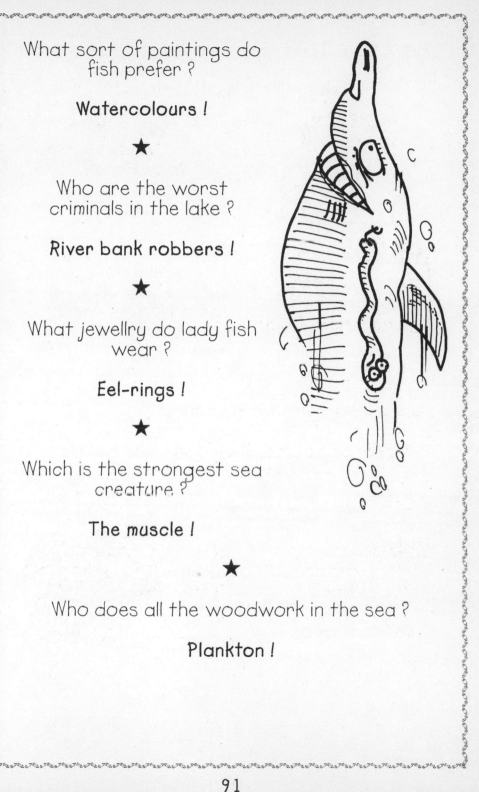

What sort of paintings do fish prefer ?

Watercolours !

★

Who are the worst criminals in the lake ?

River bank robbers !

★

What jewellry do lady fish wear ?

Eel-rings !

★

Which is the strongest sea creature ?

The muscle !

★

Who does all the woodwork in the sea ?

Plankton !

How do fish pass the long winter evenings ?

They tell each other tails !

★

What did the sea say to the beach ?

It didn't say anything - it waved !

★

Where do fish keep their savings ?

In the river bank !

★

What do you call a whale in the Sahara desert ?

Lost !

★

Which part of the fish do we eat that it doesn't actually have ?

Fish fingers !

★

Where would you find a pilot whale ?

On board a flying fish !

★

Two men were walking along in the desert. One said to the other "This is a lovely sandy beach." The other replied "Yes, but the tide is a heck of a long way out !"

"Goody," said a shark as a surfer sped by on the crest of a wave, "I love fast food!"

★

Did you know that fish mums and dads teach their children not to start eating maggots - in case they get hooked!

★

Why don't fish play tennis?

Because they always get caught up in the net!

★

What toys do baby fish play with?

Doll - fins!

★

What fish can make your feet light up?

An electric eel!

★

Batty Brain Teasers...

Why did the man order alphabet soup?

He wanted to eat his words!

★

What did the space monster say after it had eaten a planet ?

"A Mars a day helps you work, rest and play !"

★

What is the name of the detective who solves all his crimes by pure accident ?

Sheer - Luck Holmes !

★

What is the one thing you can catch with your hands tied ?

A cold !

★

Who invented the steam engine ?

No he didn't, it was Watt !

★

Why are dentists so miserable ?

Because they are always looking down in the mouth !

★

Why are men with beards more honest ?

Because they can't tell bare-faced lies !

★

What do you get if you drop a
piano down a coal mine ?

A flat minor !

★

What's the best thing to put into a pie ?

Your knife and fork !

★

Which is the strongest thing in the garden ?

The muscle sprout !

★

And which is the weakest ?

The weeds !

★

Why are teddies good at being spies ?

Because they can tell bear faced lies !

★

Waiter, there's a fly in my soup !

Don't worry, I'll give you a reduction for the soup he eats!

★

Why do elephants wear wear green jackets ?

So they can walk across a pool table without being seen !

Where would you find a rubber trumpet ?

In an elastic band !

★

Where does tea come from ?

In between the letters · S and U !

★

What starts at the bottom and goes all the way down to the floor ?

Your leg !

★

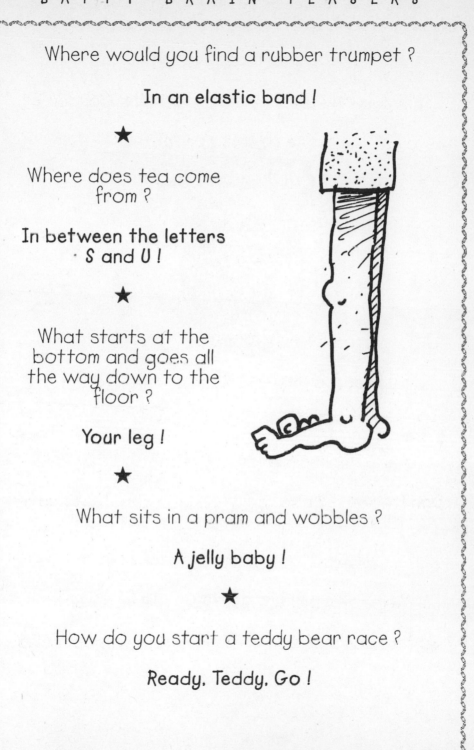

What sits in a pram and wobbles ?

A jelly baby !

★

How do you start a teddy bear race ?

Ready, Teddy, Go !

How do you make Scotch eggs ?

Feed your chickens whisky !

★

What gets bigger the more you take out of it ?

A hole !

★

How do you make a Swiss roll ?

Push him down an alp !

★

Little dog,
crossing street,
motor car,
sausage meat !

★

What sort of music was invented by cave men ?

Rock music !

★

What happened to the man who stole
a truck load of prunes ?

He was on the run for months !

★

Waiter, there's a fly in my soup !

**Thank you for telling me, sir,
I'd forgotten to put that
on the bill !**

★

How do you get rid of a boomerang ?

Throw it down a one-way street !

★

What's black and white and red all over ?

A newspaper !

How does the snow queen travel about ?

By icicle !

★

How do you get down from a giraffe ?

You don't get down from a giraffe - you get down from a duck !

★

What goes zzub, zzub ?

A bee flying backwards !

★

Why do cows moo ?

Because their horns don't work !

★

What is
Dracula's
favourite
TV game show ?

**The Crypt-on
factor !**

★

How do you make a
Venetian blind ?

Poke him in the eyes !

★

What kind of nuts do
the Russians and
Americans send into
space ?

Astronuts !

★

What sort of music do
miners like to listen to ?

Rock and coal !

★

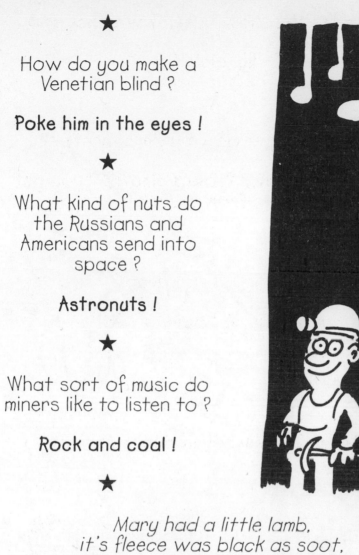

Mary had a little lamb,
it's fleece was black as soot,
and everywhere that Mary went,
its sooty foot it put !

★

What do they call the back entrance to a cafeteria ?

The bacteria !

★

What do you call the room where Inuits train their dogs ?

The mushroom !

★

Who swings from cake to cake ?

Tarzipan !

Why did the doll blush ?

Because she saw the teddy bare !

★

How do you know when it's been raining cats and dogs ?

There are lots of little poodles on the pavement !

★

What do you call a cat with 8 legs ?

An octopus !

★

What do Inuits eat for breakfast ?

Ice Crispies !

★

Where would you find a dog with 4 broken legs ?

Wherever you left it !

★

Why do potatoes always know what you've done ?

Because they have eyes !

How do carpenters go on holiday ?

They fly there by plane !

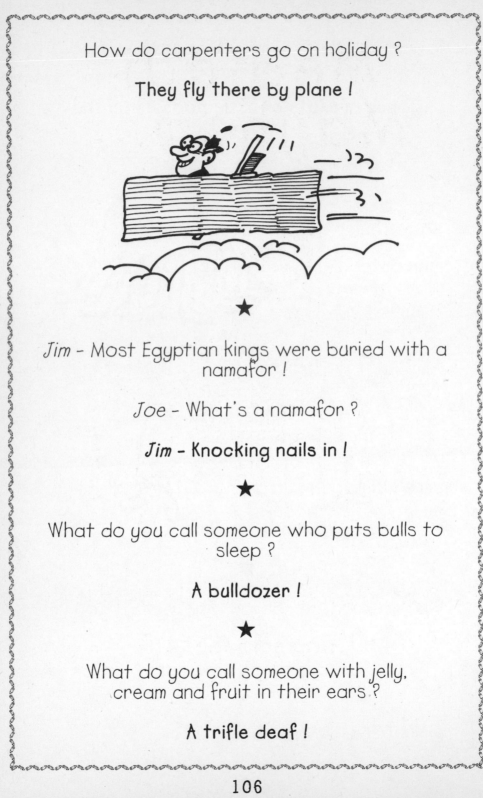

★

Jim - Most Egyptian kings were buried with a namafor !

Joe - What's a namafor ?

Jim - **Knocking nails in !**

★

What do you call someone who puts bulls to sleep ?

A bulldozer !

★

What do you call someone with jelly, cream and fruit in their ears ?

A trifle deaf !

Medical Mayhem...

Doctor, doctor, I think I'm invisible!

Who said that?

Doctor, doctor, I think I'm a pair of curtains !

Pull yourself together !

★

Doctor, doctor, my wife thinks she's a motorbike !

Give her two of these pills and she'll be cured !

But how will I get home then ?

★

Doctor, doctor, I have an inferiority complex !

Hmm. Not a very big one is it !

Doctor, doctor, I'm shrinking !

Well, you'll just have to be a little patient !

★

Doctor, doctor, my wife thinks she's a chicken !

Do you want me to cure her ?

No, I just wondered if you had any good egg recipes !

★

Doctor, doctor, everyone keeps ignoring me !

Next patient please !

★

Doctor, doctor, I think I'm a pack of cards !

You'll just have to deal with it yourself !

★

Doctor, doctor, I think I'm a mousetrap !

Snap out of it !

★

Doctor, doctor, all my friends think I'm a liar !

I find that hard to believe !

★

Doctor, doctor, I keep thinking that my parents are goats !

When did you start to have these thoughts ?

When I was a kid !

I SENT HIM HOME TO FETCH HIS NANNY!

Doctor, doctor, I think I'm becoming invisible !

I'm sorry, I can't see you now !

★

Doctor, doctor, I can't seem to get to sleep at night !

Sleep on the windowsill, you'll soon drop off !

Doctor, doctor, I have a lot of wind, can you give me anything for it?

Certainly, here's a kite!

★

Doctor, doctor, my hair is falling out, have you anything to keep it in?

Try this paper bag!

★

Doctor, doctor, you know those pills you gave me for a headache - well they worked. Now can you give me something to take the headache away!

★

Doctor, doctor, I think I'm a billiard ball!

Sorry, you'll have to go to the end of the cue!

Doctor, doctor, I keep thinking I'm a roll of film !

Don't worry, I'm sure nothing will develop !

★

Nurse, nurse, I need to see a doctor !

Which doctor?

No, just an ordinary one !

HE'S PAYING!

★

Doctor, doctor, I think I have a split personality !

In that case I will have to charge you double !

★

Doctor, doctor, I'm a little hoarse !

I'll be with you in a minute - just take your saddle off and relax !

Doctor, doctor, I swallowed a spoon !

Just sit there quietly and don't stir !

★

Doctor, doctor, I've lost my memory !

That's terrible. When did you first notice ?

When did I notice what ?

★

Doctor, doctor, I think I'm a dog !

Well, fetch this stick then roll over and let me tickle your tummy !

Will that cure me ?

No, but I was never allowed to have a pet as a child !

★

Doctor, doctor, I think I have a split personality !

I'm sorry, one of you will have to wait outside !

Doctor, doctor, my wife wants to know if you can stop me being so argumentative ?

I'm sorry Mr. Brown, there's nothing I can do !

Yes there is !

★

I'm not feeling myself today, so can you ask the doctor to call round and see Mr. Smith instead !

★

Doctor, doctor, I keep thinking that I have been here before !

Oh. It's you again !

★

Doctor, doctor, can you help me to stop smoking ?

Well, you could try not setting fire to your trousers !

★

Doctor, doctor, can you give me a sick note to get a week off school ?

You look perfectly healthy to me !

Yes, but I'm sick of going to school !

★

Doctor, doctor, I've just swallowed a tin of gloss paint !

Yes, my receptionist said you'd taken a shine to her !

★

Doctor, doctor my wife just buried my radio in the garden !

Why did she do that ?

The batteries were dead !

★

Doctor, doctor, I've got athlete's foot in my head !

What makes you think that ?

Because my nose keeps running !

★

Doctor, doctor, what's the best cure for water on the knee ?

A tap on the ankle !

★

Doctor, doctor, I have flowers growing out of the top of my head !

Don't worry, it's just a beauty spot !

★

Doctor, doctor, I think I need glasses !

I'll say you do - this is a fish and chip shop !

★

Doctor, doctor, I'm suffering from delusions of grandeur !

Sit down, your Majesty, and tell me all about it !

★

Doctor, doctor, how can I lose 15 kilos of ugly fat ?

How about cutting your head off ?

Doctor, doctor, I'm covered in spots - I need to do something about it straight away !

Now, now, let's not do anything rash !

★

Doctor, doctor, my dog has just bitten me !

In that case we will need to check for infection !

Thank you - that will put my mind at rest !

So, when can you bring the dog in?

★

Doctor, doctor, I kissed a girl and she turned into a frog !

Where is she now ?

Waiting in the croakroom !

★

Doctor, doctor, I've swallowed my pen, what should I do ?

You'll have to use a pencil !

Doctor, doctor I can't stop sneezing - what can you give me ?

A tissue ?

Oh, no, it's happening to you as well now !

★

Doctor, doctor, I'm worried. This is the first time I've had an operation !

I know how you feel - it's the first time I've done one !

★

Doctor, doctor, I get so nervous when I drive I keep bumping into things !

Don't worry I'll prescribe a crash course !

★

Doctor, doctor I've gone blind, what should I do ?

Put your crash helmet on the right way round !

★

Doctor, doctor, I've got my foot caught in a colander !

Hmm. Sounds like a strained ankle !

Crazy
Crosses...

What do you get if you cross your
mum's sister with an Inuit ?

Auntie freeze !

What do you get if you cross a kangaroo with a sheep?

A woolly jumper !

G'DAY!

★

What do you get if you cross a kangaroo with a line of people waiting for a bus ?

A queue jumper !

★

What do you get if you cross a road without looking ?

Knocked down, stupid !

★

What do you get if you cross a policeman with a landscape artist ?

A constable !

★

What do you get if you cross a fish with a children's' nanny ?

Mrs. Troutfire !

What do you get if you cross a film director and a horse drawn vehicle ?

Orson Kart !

★

What do you get if you cross a bear with a cow pat ?

Winnie the Pooh !

★

What do you get if you cross a chicken with a skunk ?

A fowl smell !

★

What do you get if you cross a fly with a detective ?

A police insector !

★

What do you get if you cross a cow with a thief ?

A beef burglar !

What do you get if you cross a pig with an ambulance ?

A Hambulance !

★

What do you get if you cross
a window cleaner with a giraffe ?

A window cleaner who doesn't
need any ladders !

★

What do you get
if you cross
a pig with Dracula
?

A Hampire !

★

What do you get if you cross a chicken
with someone who tells jokes ?

A comedihen !

What do you get if you cross a frog and a fizzy drink ?

Croaka-Cola !

★

What do you get if you cross the X files with something you keep your fuel in ?

A coal Scully !

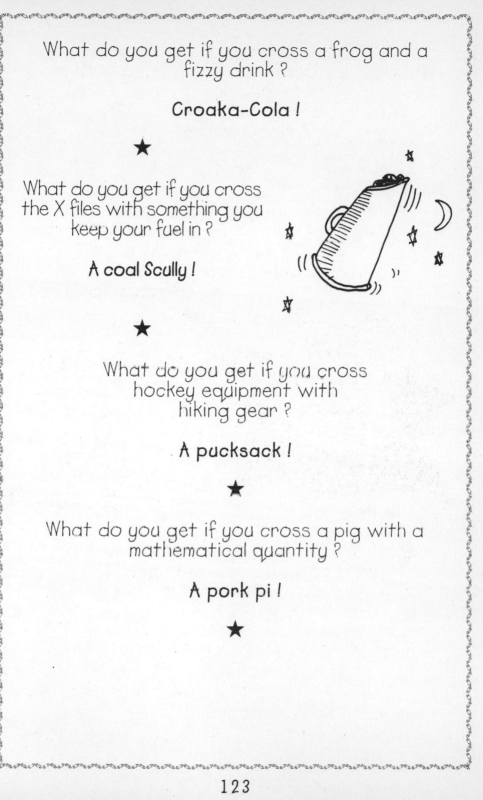

★

What do you get if you cross hockey equipment with hiking gear ?

A pucksack !

★

What do you get if you cross a pig with a mathematical quantity ?

A pork pi !

★

What do you get if you cross a goldfish
bowl with a TV ?

Tele-fish-ion !

★

What do you get if you cross an explorer with
a cat ?

Christopher Columpuss !

★

What do you get if
you cross a
cowboy with
a dinosaur ?

Tyrannosaurus Tex !

★

What do you get if you cross a pudding
with an ape ?

Lemon meringue-utan pie !

★

What do you get if you cross the mafia
and a box of teaspoons ?

A gangstir !

What do you get if you cross a river with a broken bridge ?

Very wet I should think !

★

What do you get if you cross a tree with a fruit ?

A Pineapple !

★

What do you get if you cross a math teacher with anything ?

A math teacher !

★

What do you get if you cross a pony with a TV detective ?

Inspector Horse !

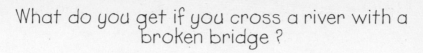

What do you get if you cross a famous detective and a lot of good fortune ?

Sheer luck Holmes !

What do you get if you cross a
cow pat and a microprocessor ?

A com-pooh-ter !

★

What do you get if you cross a mouse
and an elephant ?

An animal that's scared to look in the mirror !

★

What do you
get if you cross
a dog with
someone
worried about
something ?

Nervous Rex !

★

What do you get if you cross a duck and
a TV programme ?

A Duckumentary !

★

What do you get if you cross garden birds
with a famous aerobatic display team ?

The Red Sparrows !

★

What do you get if you cross two rows of
cabbages with a main road?

A dual cabbageway !

★

What do you get if
you cross kitchen
equipment with a
vampire ?

Count spatula !

★

What do you get if
you cross a giant ape
with an aeroplane ?

King Kongcorde !

★

What do you get if you cross a spy and a duvet ?

An under-cover agent !

★

What do you get if you cross a cat and an octopus ?

A cat-o-nine-tails !

★

What do you get if you cross a pop group with a ton of latex ?

A rubber band !

★

What do you get if you cross a cow pat with a boomerang ?

A nasty smell you can't get rid of !

★

What do you get if you cross dandruff
and a French fried potato ?

A chip on your shoulder !

★

What do you get if you cross a
stick of dynamite and a pig ?

Bangers !

★

What do you get if
you cross a giraffe
and a cow ?

**Something you need a
ladder to milk !**

★

What do you get if
you cross a
traffic warden with a
dog ?

A barking ticket !

★

What do you get if you cross a coal mine
with a cow ?

A pit - bull !

★

What do you get if you cross a cow with
a CD player ?

Pop - Moosic !

★

What do you get if you mislay your violin
in a match factory ?

Fiddlesticks !

★

What do you get if you cross a fox
with a carrot ?

Something that no rabbit will dare to steal
from the vegetable patch !

★

What do you get if you put a car engine into
an old sailing ship ?

About 45 miles to the galleon !

Holiday Howlers...

Our math teacher is going
to the Bahamas this *Summer* !

Jamaica ?

No, she wanted to go !

★

When we went on holiday last year - the aeroplane was so old...

...it had solid tires !

...the 2 previous owners were the Wright Brothers !

...one of the seats said "Reserved for Julius Caesar" !

...the co-pilot had to keep running to the tail to rewind the motor !

...the seats were covered in dinosaur hide !

...the pilot was taught to fly by Baron Von Richtofen !

★

Who always gets the sack on his first day at work ?

Santa Claus !

★

★

Dear Santa...

If I'm good
it's understood
that you'll bring me
a new CD.

If I'm kind
I know I'll find
a guitar to play
on Christmas Day.

So from now on,
You're going to find,
that I'll be helpful,
good and kind,
and I intend to stay
that way !
At least, that is, till
Boxing day !

★

Passenger- I'm nervous, I've never flown before ?

**Hostess- Oh, don't you start, I've got enough
trouble with the pilot !**

★

What do you call two girls with Christmas
decorations on their heads ?

Holly and Ivy !

★

Where do snowmen go
to dance ?

Snowballs !

★

What do you call
someone who casts
spells at the seaside ?

A Sandwitch !

★

*Two elephants wanted to go swimming at
the seaside but they couldn't - they only
had one pair of trunks between them !*

★

What do you call a man with a
bucket and spade on his head ?

Doug !

★

How did you find your steak sir?

Easy. I just moved these two chips and there it was!

★

Waiter ! This egg is bad !

That's not my fault. I only laid the table !

★

How does a vampire cross the channel to France ?

In a blood vessel !

★

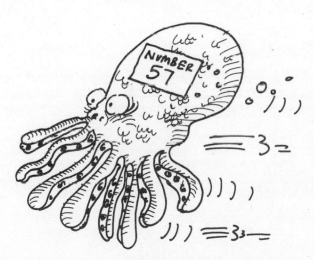

How do fish go on holiday ?

By octobus !

★

What sort of clothes do people wear
in very hot countries ?

Blazers !

★

Where are the Andes ?

On the ends of your armies !

★

Why do birds fly South in the Winter ?

It's too far to walk !

★

When bees go on holiday where do
they wait for the coach ?

At a buzz stop !

★

What is grey, has four legs and a trunk ?

A mouse going on holiday !

★

Why did the elephant wear sunglasses on the beach ?

Because he didn't want to be recognised !

★

A witch wanted to go on a
motor cycling holiday...

**...so she bought a
brrooommm stick !**

★

"Good morning ladies and gentlemen. Welcome aboard the World's first ever fully computerised aeroplane. There is no need for a pilot or co-pilot on this aircraft, as everything is fully automated. We are currently flying at 30,000 feet and everything is working perfectly...working porfectly...burking lurfectly...smirking carpetly..."

★

What flavour chips
can you use to take
you on holiday ?

Plane !

Where do school dinner ladies go on holiday ?

Greece !

★

Why do policemen like to go to
discos when they are on holiday ?

They really enjoy the beat !

★

What's big and grey and flies you to
your holiday destination ?

A jumbo jet !

★

*Three friends went on a cruise holiday, but
were shipwrecked on a desert island. A good
fairy came and gave them one wish each. The
first two men wished they were back at home
with their families. The third man thought for
a minute and said , "It's quiet around here all
on my own, I wish my two friends were still
here with me !"*

★

Did you hear about the elephant who couldn't
go on holiday - the notice said that all cases,
bags and trunks had to go through the
airport X-Ray machine !

Waiter - do you have frog's legs ?

Yes, monsieur !

Well, hop into the kitchen and get me a steak !

★

Tourist-Do you have a room for the night ?

Hotelier-Certainly, sir. $100 a night or $20 a night if you make your own bed.

Tourist - I'll take the $20 room please !

Hotelier - Fine. You'll find the wood in the room and I'll bring the hammer and nails up in a minute !

★

What do jelly babies travel in on holiday ?

A jelly copter !

★

Where do monks go for a break ?

Holy-Day camps !

★

Two friends had enjoyed a great days
fishing on a lake.

*"We must come here again," said one,
"but how will we ever find this same spot
on such a huge lake?"*

**"No problem," said his friend, "I've marked
an X on the side of the boat !"**

★

What do cave men do on holiday ?

They go out night-clubbing !

★

How do cave men afford holidays ?

They club together !

★

Mirthful Miscellany...

Did you hear about the girl who
fell asleep with her head
under the pillow...

...the fairies came and
took out all her teeth !

★

Where has all the lemonade gone. I though we agreed to have half the bottle each ?

We did - my half was the bottom half, and I had to drink yours to get to it !

★

Cannibal 1 - I don't know what to make of my children these days ? !

Cannibal 2 - How about curry !

★

Doctor, doctor, my little boy has swallowed all the coins from my purse !

Don't worry - the change will probably do him good !

★

Dad, am I worth a million dollars to you ?

Of course you are, son !

In that case can you lend me $20 of it now, I want to go to the cinema !

★

★

Where does a vampire keep his money ?

In a bank a - Count !

★

What is made from fruit, served with custard and
moan all the time you're eating it ?

Apple grumble !

★

Where does a monster relax on holiday ?

On a ghoulf course !

★

Why was the policeman offered a job
on the buses ?

Because copper is such a good conductor !

★

What did the burglar say to the blonde
policeman who caught him breaking into
a big top ?

It's a fair cop, fair cop !

★

Did you hear about the policeman who was invited to join the Royal Shakespeare Company...

...he always gave an arresting performance !

★

What does a policeman call an overdue library fine ?

An old bill !

★

What goes ' ello, ello, tick, tock, woof, ello, ello, tick, tock, woof...'

A police watchdog !

★

What goes 'ho, ho, ho, ho, clonk'

Someone laughing their head off !

★

Why do witches fly around on broomsticks ?

Because vacuum cleaners don't have long enough cords !

★

What do you call a stupid vampire ?
A blood clot !

What did the policeman say to his tummy ?

I've got you under a vest !

★

What do you do if your nose goes on strike ?

Picket !

★

What tables can't you eat ?

Vegetables !

★

Why do bicycles never do anything exciting ?

Because they are always two tired !

★

What do you have to know before you can start training a pet ?

More than the pet !

★

What comes after the letter A ?

The rest of the alphabet !

★

How do you lift an elephant

Sit him on an acorn and wait for it to grow !

★

I would tell you the joke about the bed...

...but it hasn't been made up yet !

★

What is red on the outside and grey
and crowded on the inside ?

A bus full of elephants !

★

What does an elephant
do when it rains ?

Gets wet !

★

How do you stop your dog barking in the back of the car ?

Put it in the front !

★

What is worse than finding a maggot when you bite into an apple ?

Finding half of one !

★

What is brown and sticky ?

A stick !

★

What is green and bouncy ?

A spring onion !

★

Why do wizards drink so much tea ?

Because sorcerers need cuppas !

★

How do you cut through the waves ?

With a sea-saw !

★

What sort of nuts
sneeze the most ?

Cashews !

★

What musical device
follows a bee ?

C D !

★

Why did the owl make
everyone laugh ?

**Because he was a
hoot !**

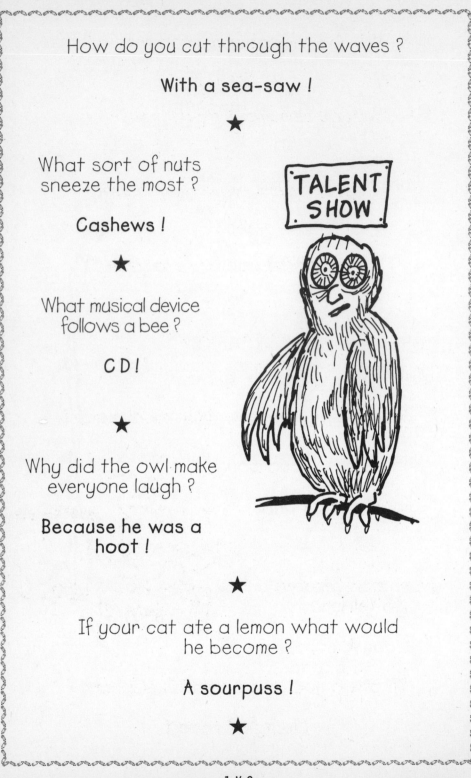

★

If your cat ate a lemon what would
he become ?

A sourpuss !

★

Will you remember me tomorrow ?

Yes !

Will you remember me next week ?

Yes !

Will you remember me next month ?

Yes !

Will you remember me in a year ?

Yes !

Knock, knock

Who's there ?

You see, you've forgotten me already !

★

Knock Knock...
Who's there ?
Ivor...
Ivor who ?
**Ivor good mind not
to tell you !**

★

What do you give a seasick elephant ?

Plenty of room !

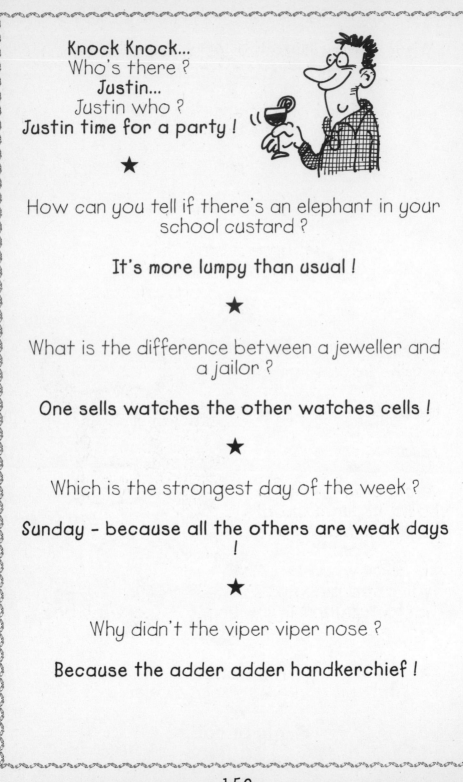

Knock Knock...
Who's there ?
Justin...
Justin who ?
Justin time for a party !

★

How can you tell if there's an elephant in your school custard ?

It's more lumpy than usual !

★

What is the difference between a jeweller and a jailor ?

One sells watches the other watches cells !

★

Which is the strongest day of the week ?

Sunday - because all the others are weak days !

★

Why didn't the viper viper nose ?

Because the adder adder handkerchief !

What is the difference between a fisherman
and an idle schoolboy ?

**One baits hooks, the other
hates books !**

★

Why did the jam roll ?

**Because it saw the
apple turnover !**

★

Two cows were
talking in a field..

*first cow - 'Are you
worried about this
mad cow disease ?'*

**second cow - 'Why
should I worry about
that - I'm a penguin !'**

★

What do you get if you cross a snowman and a
mosquito ?

Frostbite !

★

★

What zooms along the bed of the lake ?

A motor pike and side carp !

★

Why shouldn't you complain about
the price of a train ticket ?

Because it's bound to be fare !

★

How do you tell which end
of a worm is the head ?

**Tickle it in the middle and see
which end laughs !**

★

Romeo - Do you love me ?

Juliet - Of course I do !

Romeo - Then whisper something soft and
sweet.

Juliet - **Lemon Meringue Pie !**

★

★

I'll teach you to throw stones at my greenhouse !

I wish you would - I keep missing !

★

Did you hear about the man who was hit on the head with a pan full of curry ?

He ended up in a Korma !

★

There were two bishops in a bed - which one wore the nightie ?

Mrs. Bishop !

★

What happens when pigs fly ?

The price of bacon goes up !

★

Why did the tap dancer have to retire ?

He kept falling into the sink !

★

What is the difference between a nail
and a bad boxer ?

**One gets knocked in, the other gets
knocked out !**

★

How many ears has Captain Kirk ?

**Three ! A right ear, a left ear and a
final frontier !**

★

How does a chimpanzee make toast ?

Puts it under the gorilla !

★

What do jelly babies
wear in the rain ?

Gum boots !

★

What is small, green
and goes camping ?

A boy sprout !

What does a Swedish Fred Flintstone shout ?

Abba dabba Doo !

★

What do you get when you cross a jelly with a sheep dog ?

Collie wobbles !

★

What kind of ears does a train have ?

Engineers !

★

Why was the farmer hopping mad ?

Because someone trod on his corn !

★

Blenkinsop- why have you brought a fish into music class ?

You said we were going to play scales today, sir !

Why is a farmer cruel ?

Because he pulls corn by its ears !

★

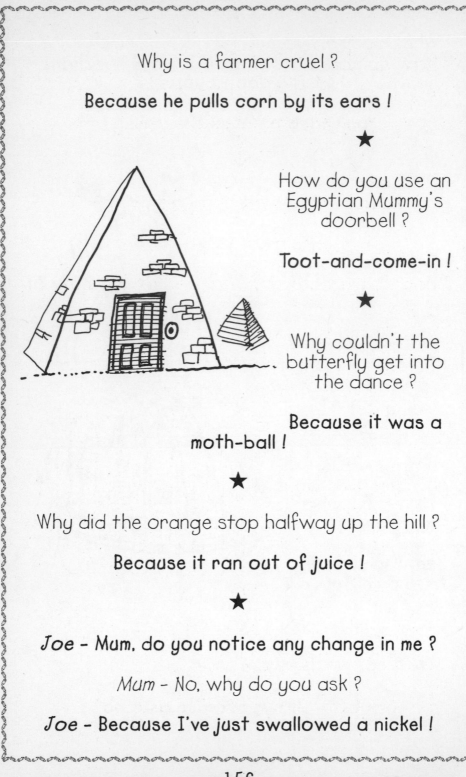

How do you use an
Egyptian Mummy's
doorbell ?

Toot-and-come-in !

★

Why couldn't the
butterfly get into
the dance ?

**Because it was a
moth-ball !**

★

Why did the orange stop halfway up the hill ?

Because it ran out of juice !

★

Joe - Mum, do you notice any change in me ?

Mum - No, why do you ask ?

Joe - Because I've just swallowed a nickel !

How do you know when there's an elephant hiding under your bed ?

Your nose touches the ceiling !

★

Waiter, waiter, what do you call this ?

It's bean soup sir !

I don't care what it's been - what is it now ? !

★

I would tell you the joke about the butter - but you would only spread it !

★

And - I would tell you the joke about the fence - but I know you would never get over it !

★

Dracula's School Report

Reading - Good
Writing - Average
Cricket - shows promise as a bat !

What did Tarzan say when he saw the elephants coming over the hill ?

Here come the elephants !

★

What shoot along the washing line at 70 miles an hour?

Hondapants !

★

How can you keep cool at a football match ?

Stand next to a fan !

★

What do you get if you cross a crocodile with a rose ?

I don't know but I wouldn't try smelling it !

★

Who did Dracula marry ?

The girl necks door !

★

Did you hear about the two flies playing football in the saucer - they were practising for the cup !

★

What did the baby chicken say when his mum laid a jar of orange jam ?

Ooh ! Look what marmalade !

★

Shall I tell you the joke about the box of corn flakes ?

I hope you've got plenty of time - It's a cereal !

★

How do you keep an idiot in suspense ?

I'll tell you tomorrow !

★

Where do monsters stay on holiday ?

In a bed-for-breakfast hotel !

★

What is the difference between an African elephant and an Indian elephant ?

African elephants can't cook curry !

★

What sort of car does a farmer's dog drive ?

A Range Rover !

★

Did you hear about the burglar who was arrested in his shower - he was trying to make a clean getaway !

★

How do you make a cake stand ?

Hide all the chairs !

★

Policeman - You just went through a red light !

Motorist - Sorry, blame it on my good manners. My mum taught me never to look when someone was changing !

And always remember that before you give someone a piece of your mind, make sure you can manage on what you have left !

★

What sort of shoes can you make from banana skins ?

Slippers !

★

Jim – My sister married an Irishman !

Joe – Oh. Really ?

Jim – **No. O'Reilly !**

★

Woodwork teacher – What are you making ?

Pupil – A portable.

Woodwork teacher – A portable what ?

Pupil – **I don't know yet – I only just made the handle !**

★

Mum – Why haven't you changed the water in the goldfish bowl ?

Daughter – **Because they haven't drunk the first lot yet !**

What do you do with a sick budgie ?

Send it for tweetment !

★

Your teeth are like stars...

(they come out at night)

Your cheeks are like petals...

(bicycle petals)

★

What are those little bongos dangling from your ears ?

They're my ear drums !

★

Did you hear about the man who went to the doctor and told him he thought he was a suitcase ?

The doctor sent him packing !

★

What do you get if you cross a pig with a flea ?

Pork scratchings !

★

Which of Tarzan's underwear swing through the trees ?

Junglepants !

★

Why is a bull that has swallowed a hand grenade like a yeti ?

They are both abominable !

★

Now for some composers...

Which composer can't you find ?

Haydn !

Which composer can help you with the shopping ?

Liszt !

Which composer sounds like a dog ?

Bach !

★

A man walked into a bar. What did he say?

OOf! It was an iron bar!

★

Why is it dangerous to tell jokes when you're skating?

Because the ice might crack up!

★

Sickly smiles...

What do you call a bird that
falls under a lawn mower ?

Shredded tweet !

★

After the monster had bitten off both my legs the police refused to arrest him !

Why was that ?

They said he had no arm in him !

★

What's green and hairy and has 18 legs ?

I don't know !

Neither do I, but it's just crawled up into your shorts !

★

Why did the chicken cross the road ?

I don't know !

It was going for an eye test, which explains why it got hit by a bus !

★

What did the bus conductor say to the monster with 3 heads, no arms and 1 leg ?

Hello, hello, hello you look armless, hop on !

★

★

Doctor - Stand in front
of the window and
stick out your tongue.

Patient -Are you going
to examine it ?

**Doctor -No, I just
don't like the man who
lives in the house
opposite !**

★

What do you call a
deer with its eyes
poked out ?

No eye deer !

★

What do you call a dead deer with its eyes
poked out ?

Still no eye deer !

★

★

Those toffees were nice - but why were they furry ?

My mum sucked them up into the vacuum cleaner !

★

Why was the monster eating a horse in his bedroom at two in the morning ?

He was having a night mare !

★

What's yellow, sticky and smells of bananas ?

Monkey sick !

What's the first thing a monster eats after he's had his teeth checked by the dentist ?

The dentist !

★

Where do you find monster snails ?

On the end of monsters' fingers !

★

Waiter - why is there a frog in my soup ?

To catch the flies !

★

★

Waiter, why have you got your thumb in my soup ?

I have a boil on my thumb and the doctor said I have to keep it warm !

★

What's the best thing to do with a green monster ?

Wait until he's ripe or you'll get tummy ache after eating him !

★

Did you hear about the really stupid woodworm ?

It was found dead in a housebrick !

★

What is green and white and swings through the trees ?

Tarzan's handkerchief !

★

★

What is black and white and red at the bottom ?

A baby zebra with diaper rash !

★

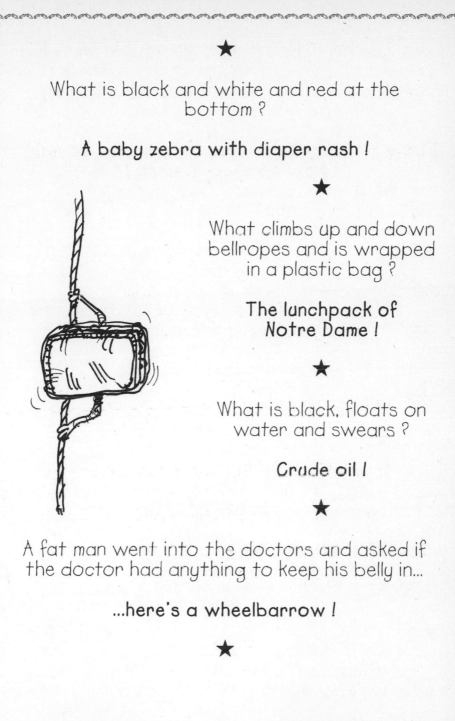

What climbs up and down bellropes and is wrapped in a plastic bag ?

The lunchpack of Notre Dame !

★

What is black, floats on water and swears ?

Crude oil !

★

A fat man went into the doctors and asked if the doctor had anything to keep his belly in...

...here's a wheelbarrow !

★

Jim - If there are ten flies on a table and I kill one with a newspaper, how many will be left ?

Joe - Only the dead one !

★

What vegetable do you never want to see in a boat ?

A leek !

★

Who is that at the door ?

A man with a wooden leg.

Tell him to hop it !

★

Did you hear about the man with two wooden legs who caught fire ?

He burned down to the ground !

★

A little boy took a bucket into the living room and put it down in front of his elderly granny. He asked her to kick it - "'cos then my dad says we'll have plenty of money and I can have a new bike !"

What do you call...?

What do you call a Scottish
cloak room attendant ?

Willie Angus McCoatup !

★

What do you call a man with a calculator on his head ?

Adam !

★

What do call a place where aliens go to see films?

Cine- Mars !

★

What is a rodent's favourite sport ?

Ka-rat-e !

★

What do you call someone with a pair of shoes on their head ?

A sole singer !

★

What do call a man with 6 arms ?

Andy !

★

What do you call the young lady who lives in the coffin next to dracula's ?

The ghoul next door !

★

What do you call a man with a duck on his head ?

Quackers !

★

What do you call a small horse following somcone ?

A Pony tail !

★

What do you call a frog who can leave his car anywhere ?

A Parking Kermit !

★

What do you call the college that a parrot goes to ?

A Polly-technic !

★

What do you call a man who can sing and drink lemonade at the same time ?

A pop singer !

★

What do you call a cat that is always having accidents ?

A catastrophe !

★

What do you call a machine for counting cows ?

A cowculator !

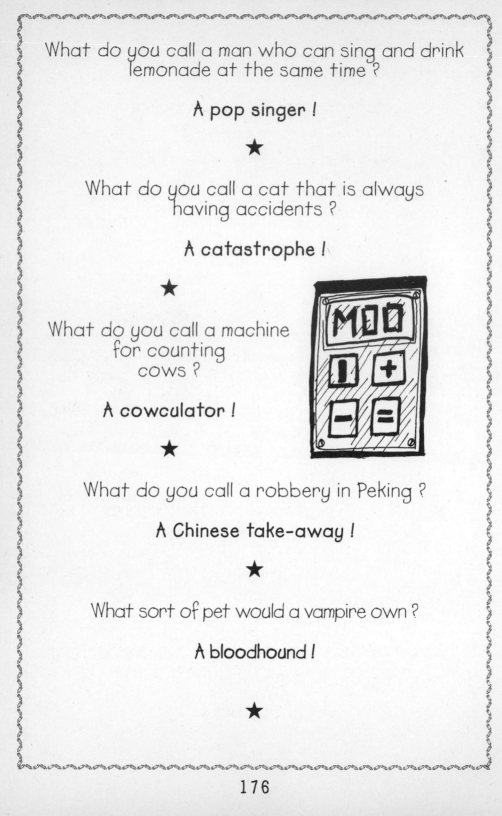

★

What do you call a robbery in Peking ?

A Chinese take-away !

★

What sort of pet would a vampire own ?

A bloodhound !

★

Why couldn't the executioner decide what job he wanted to do?

He kept chopping and changing!

★

What do you call the man who writes all Dracula's jokes?

His crypt writer!

★

What do you call the shark who does impersonations of one of the Beatles?

Jaws Harrison!

★

What do you call work that fairies have to do after school?

Gnomework!

★

What do you call a streetlight where monsters hang around waiting for victims?

A ghoulpost!

What do you call the carpet cleaner that vampires use ?

A victim cleaner !

★

What do you call it when your teacher is having a baby ?

A Miss-conception !

★

What do you call a spanner belonging to a toad ?

A toad's tool !

★

What do you call the place where cats have fashion shows ?

Catwalks !

★

What do you call a dead parrot ?

A Polygon !

★

★

What do you call a Tibetan chicken ?

Himalaya !

★

What do you call someone who doesn't use a hanky ?

Greensleeves !

★

What do you call a prisoner's pet budgie ?

A jailbird !

★

What do you call it when someone tries to rob a bank with a bunch of flowers ?

Robbery with violets !

★

What do you call the largest mouse in the World ?

Hippopotamouse !

★

What do you call it when you pick up the phone and send elephants charging in the opposite direction ?

A reverse-charge call !

★

What do you call a Teddy bear's favourite drink ?

Ginger bear !

★

What do you call the skeleton who was once the Emperor of France ?

Napoleon Boney Parts !

★

What do you call a cat that works in a hospital ?

A first aid kit !

★

What do you call a cat that plays the drums ?

A drum kit !

★

What do you call a cat that makes models ?

A construction kit !

★

What do you call a snake that grabs a cricketer ?

A bowler constrictor !

★

What do you call the last man to abandon ship ?

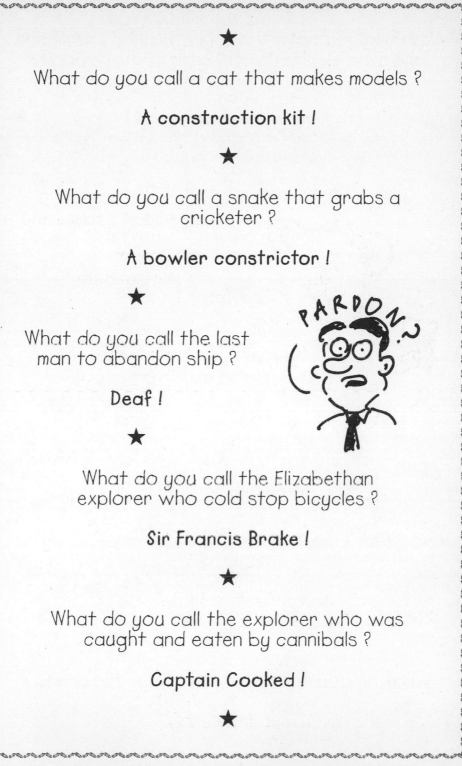

Deaf !

★

What do you call the Elizabethan explorer who cold stop bicycles ?

Sir Francis Brake !

★

What do you call the explorer who was caught and eaten by cannibals ?

Captain Cooked !

★

What do you call a man with a toilet on his head ?

John !

(Of course he might have two if he was feeling flush !)

★

What do you call twin brothers, each with a drum on his head ?

Tom, Tom !

★

What do you call a cat in a panic ?

Cat flap !

★

What do you call the biggest ant in the World ?

An elephant !

★

What do you call a house where Martians live ?

A greenhouse !

★

What did the Martian say to the gas pump ?

**Take your finger out of your ear
when I'm talking to you !**

★

What do you call a dog that likes doing
experiments ?

A Lab-rador !

★

What do you call the stuff your milkman delivers
if you live at the end of a two mile cobbled
street ?

Yogurt !

★

What do you call the dance where all cakes are
invited ?

Abundance !

★

What do you call it when two cows
munch grass side by side to keep warm ?

Double grazing !

★

What do you call a sheep dog when
it has eaten too much melon ?

Melancholy !

★

What do you call a highly dangerous cake ?

Atilla the bun !

★

What do you call the cake that was served
after the battle of the Little Big Horn ?

Custer's slices !

★

What do you call a cake you can use to
power your portable CD ?

Current cake !

★

What do you call a cake you can give to mice ?

Cheesecake !

★

What do you call a cake you eat in the bath ?

Sponge !

★

What do you call a dog that likes wrapping presents ?

A boxer !

★

What do you call a madman who has a wash then runs away ?

Nut, washes and bolts !

★

What do you call the children of the Tsar of Russia ?

Tsar- dines !

★

What do you call a chimney built upside down ?

A well !

★

What do you call the most unhealthy bird ?

The Puffin !

★

What do you call the pliers you use in maths ?

Multipliers !

★

★ What do you call a nickel that can't go to the toilet ?

Coin-stipated !

★

What do you call stupid flowers that grow in a pond ?

Water sillies !

★

What do you call a sheep with fangs ?

A Lamb-pire !

★

What do you call a Shakespearian actor who eats garlic ?

Mac Breath !

★

Final Fling...

Whose daddy was a mummy ?

Tutankhamen !

Joe - Last night I opened the door in my pyjamas !

Jim - Why on earth have you got a door in your pyjamas ?

★

What do you call a bird drinking two drinks at once ?

Toucan !

★

Did you hear about the monster who ate a settee and two chairs for lunch ?

He had a three piece suite tooth !

★

Mum, can you help me with my maths homework, I'm trying to find the lowest common denominator ?

Crickey, they were trying to find that when I was at school !

★

Why did the fly fly ?

Because the spider spied her !

What do you get if you cross
a pig with a dinosaur ?

Jurassic Pork!

★

When the monster had finished his tea he
asked his mum if he could leave the table.

**She said yes he could, as long as
he had eaten the chairs!**

★

Did you hear about the stupid burglar who
threw two bricks through the jewellers
window...

**...Because someone told him they had double
glazing!**

★

Which snake tells tales ?

The grass snake!

★

What do you call an environmentally friendly,
noiseless, biodegradable food mixer that uses
no electricity ?

A wooden spoon!

How do you stop a mouse from squeaking ?

Oil it !

★

Which two kings were good at fractions ?

Richard the third and Henry the eighth !

★

Who was the first man on the moon ?

A spaceman !

★

What lies under your bed at night with its tongue hanging out ?

Your shoe !

Why was the cat lying on the toast rack ?

It was a marmalade cat !

★

What would happen to a penguin in the desert ?

The chocolate would melt !

★

Have you heard about the boy who kept a pencil in his bedroom...

...so he could draw the curtains every morning !

★

*Little Miss Muffet
sat on a tuffet,
eating tandoori and rice.
A monster from Bury
ate Miss Muffet and curry,
and said 'by golly that was nice !'*

★

Teacher - Name three birds that can't fly.

Pupil - An ostrich and two dead sparrows !

★